THE
Archive Photographs
SERIES
STONEHOUSE
THE STANLEYS
AND SELSLEY

THE ROYAL VISIT TO SELSLEY. On Monday 21 April 1941, Queen Mary, who spent much of the war at Badminton, visited the widowed Lady Marling. Her tour of the estate included the gardens, where she saw the fountain playing, and the church. Whilst at Selsley she was introduced to P.C. Webber of Kings Stanley, for two years orderly to the late King George V. She left sharp at 6p.m. Conspicuous at the gate, we are told, was a 'chubby little lad wearing a red, white and blue turban and vigorously waving a Union Jack'. Her Majesty is seen here at the main entrance to the house, together with Lady Marling and Mr S.S. Marling, her brother-in-law, who lived to be nearly 99 years old. The photograph was intended as a present and is personally signed by Lady Marling.

Previous page: ERNEST SPRATT'S HORSE BUS SETTING OUT FOR KINGS STANLEY. Ernest Spratt's carrier's business served Kings Stanley, Leonard Stanley and Frocester, linking them twice daily with Stroud, where this superb photograph was taken near the Royal George Hotel in King Street. Mrs Love is the passenger second from the left. The horse bus shown, with Mr Spratt holding the reins, was used from Monday to Thursday. On Fridays and Saturdays a larger vehicle was employed.

THE
Archive Photographs
SERIES

STONEHOUSE
THE STANLEYS
AND SELSLEY

Compiled by
Howard Beard

CHALFORD

First published 1996
Copyright © Howard Beard, 1996

The Chalford Publishing Company
St Mary's Mill, Chalford,
Stroud, Gloucestershire, GL6 8NX

ISBN 0 7524 0695 7

Typesetting and origination by
The Chalford Publishing Company
Printed in Great Britain by
Redwood Books, Trowbridge

Front cover illustration:
SELSLEY SCHOOLCHILDREN, c. 1908.

WYCLIFFE COLLEGE, STONEHOUSE. This photograph has a handwritten caption: 'On a Thursday, Autumn 1906. Going out to football.'

4

VILLAGE WEDDING, SELSLEY, *c.* 1920. This fine picture is from the Cooke family collection.

Contents

CRICKET MATCH, SEPTEMBER 1911, PLAYED BETWEEN W. BARNARD'S XI AND THAT OF MISS C.M. JENNER DAVIES OF STONEHOUSE.

Introduction

When the idea for a study of the area to the west of Stroud through the medium of early photographs was first suggested, it seemed logical to consider all the villages from Arlingham to Cainscross, through Frampton-on-Severn and Stonehouse. Happily this plan had to be modified owing to the sheer volume of good photographs available, and it was eventually decided to concentrate on Stonehouse, the Stanleys and Selsley. However, even with this restriction, more than 600 possible images were examined and finally whittled down to the 200 or so required. This was both rewarding, since so much good material came to light, and also frustrating, because inevitably many good photographs had to be omitted.

The four parishes chosen were selected for two principal reasons. Firstly, they offer a varied contrast: Stonehouse has a sizeable population, with a good mix of shops and industry, and has recently acquired official town status; the Stanleys are strongly rural in character; Selsley, on the other hand, is a parish of relatively recent foundation, largely the creation of the Marling family, whose mansion and estate dominated its social life up to the start of the 1940s.

LEONARD STANLEY METHODIST CHAPEL ANNIVERSARY, *c.* 1930.

Secondly, a wealth of good postcard and private photograph collections exist in all four parishes: their owners have invariably been interested, informative and helpful.

As far as possible, material used in this book is previously unpublished, though in some instances I have used pictures already in print – for example the harvesting scene at Middleyard –simply because they are too good to omit. Photographs range in date from 1870 to the 1960s, though, mainly because the craze for collecting picture postcards peaked between 1902 and 1914, there is a predominance of images from that period.

The subject matter of the photographs is largely topographical, comprising street scenes, landscapes and events. In addition some family portraits have been included if they feature persons well-known within a particular community, or demonstrate aspects of period costume, social history or rural life. Occasionally the messages on the reverse of postcards have been quoted, if they throw light on the lives of their writers, or are simply amusing: for example, 'Thank you for your birthday present, a cake, a ball and a sixpence.' These little verbal asides provide fascinating insights into the preoccupations, concerns and pleasures of our forebears almost a century ago.

So what do both messages and photographs tell us about society at the turn of the century? Certainly the even tenor of village life had altered little in decades. The development of canals in the late eighteenth century and of railways in the 1840s provided the last major causes of change – the internal combustion engine had yet to make its impact. Horse buses still

HARVESTING, c. 1910. Taken by a Stonehouse photographer, this atmospheric village harvesting scene is thought to relate to the Stanleys.

connected village with market town. The social life of the parish centred around church, chapel, pub and workplace. Annual highlights were religious festivals or secular events such as the Stonehouse Flower Show. Healthcare was primitive – though it should be noted that Stonehouse National School became, in 1901, the first in the county where a local general practitioner examined the children each term. Poverty was rife, employment chancy, life expectancy often frighteningly short – with infant mortality still high, forty was a good average life span – yet, both from photographic and oral records, it is apparent that people were no less contented than today. A highly-developed sense of community and interdependence in adversity appear to have compensated for hardship. Family bonds were strong. Issues of law and order were more simply understood and rarely questioned. Summary justice was expected and accepted: 'apple-scrogging' merited a clipped ear from farmer or local constable, reinforced by a repeat performance if the offender's father heard of his son's misdemeanour. Pride in one's home, garden, school and village was taken for granted and led to the intense, though largely peaceful, inter-parish rivalry we see depicted in football matches, horticultural shows and carnivals. Local newspaper archives of the period have provided a fascinating and rewarding source of much vital background material. Edwardian journalistic language is flowery, extravagant, even bombastic and, to late-twentieth century ears, can sound unintentionally amusing. Yet we should understand it as an expression of the ordered, optimistic world in which people then lived. However, ahead and unsuspected, lay war, social upheaval and technological advances, which were soon to sweep away for ever this cosy, apparently permanent, way of life.

One
Stonehouse

HIGH STREET, STONEHOUSE, *c.* 1908. On the extreme left of this busy picture is the Stonehouse branch of the Cainscross and Ebley Co-operative Society. Next door, and below the sign advertising Gardiner's Cycle Works, are the premises of Frederick Restall, who was responsible for many of Stonehouse's finest Edwardian photographs. These he sold at 2 for $1\frac{1}{2}$d, 12 for 6d or 30 for 1s. Mr Restall also ground knives, razors and scissors, repaired or recovered umbrellas, sold pipes and tobacco and cut hair – clearly a man of varied talents. Beyond the ivy-covered building is the butcher's shop of F. and J. Cox, who lived at Horsemarling Farm.

Stonehouse was, until the nineteenth century, mainly a rural parish, though the proximity of the River Frome had ensured the successful development of cloth mills. By 1900 the population of Stonehouse was just over 2,000. Its position at the entrance to the Stroud valleys system had resulted in a relatively sophisticated transport network across the parish: in the 1720s two main roads had been turnpiked; shortly afterwards sections of the River Frome were made navigable to Severn trows; in the late eighteenth century the Stroudwater Canal was opened and by the 1840s both the Great Western and the Midland Railway companies had reached Stonehouse. A Midland branch line to Nailsworth opened in 1867.

Further prosperity had come in 1882 with the foundation of an independent school, Wycliffe College. Increased employment resulted, in 1890, from the opening of the Stonehouse Brick and Tile Company. Around this period, Doverow Hill, onto which the company's land backed, was given to the local Board of Health for the recreational use of the public.

It is probable that a church existed at the time of the Domesday Survey, although the entry for 'Stanhus' does not specify one. The church has an unusual dedication to St Cyr and its first recorded incumbent was listed in 1225. By 1900 Stonehouse also boasted a Congregational Chapel, founded in 1820, a Baptist Meeting House and a Methodist Chapel, erected in Regent Street in 1889.

By 1910 two banks had opened branches in the High Street, the Capital and Counties and the National Provincial, and there was also a post office. The Cottagers' Horticultural Society organised the principal social events of the year, the Flower Show and Industrial Exhibition. Two fairs were held, in May and October. Arthur Winterbotham was Lord of the Manor, and his residence was Stonehouse Court, which had recently been rebuilt after a serious fire. It is now a hotel.

Apart from the usual range of tradesmen – butchers, wheelwrights, chimney sweeps, etc. – Stonehouse also supported, more unusually, a herbalist and a marine store dealer. Jeptha Young, a self-taught poet working in Kings Stanley during the third quarter of the nineteenth century, wrote quaintly in his poem, 'Selsley Hill':

> Near Stonehouse church a river's seen
> Rolling through meadows large and green
> To join the Severn Tides.
> Near to its banks are brooks and ponds
> With Stonehouse Mill and Beard's and Bond's
> And many more besides.

HIGH STREET, AN EDWARDIAN VIEW. This picture must have been taken on the day of the Flower Show, or some other major local festivity, since the High Street is crowded with people in their best clothes and all obviously heading in the same direction. On the extreme right is the Petty Sessional Court.

LOWER REGENT STREET. Taken from a postcard, this view in Regent Street remains relatively unchanged today. The message on the reverse of the card intriguingly informs us that 'the double doors on the left is where Mr Davies had his mishap...'

AN EXCURSION BY HORSEBRAKE. In this atmospheric picture dating from around the period of World War One, a horsebrake can be seen outside the Nag's Head Inn in Regent Street. The building is still standing and is now known as 'Wayfarer's Cottage'.

QUEEN'S ROAD. The left side of Queen's Road remains much the same nowadays, though the wall and fence opposite have since been replaced by a row of wooden-framed shops and the post office. The lamp marks the entrance to the Baptist Church, which later became the British Legion Club and is now a snooker hall.

BUILDING WORK IN QUEEN'S ROAD. One of the shops mentioned above is seen here under construction. On the left a part of A.R. Blick's builder's and undertaker's yard is visible. The pair of semi-detached houses is in St Cyril's Road.

PEARCROFT ROAD, c. 1905. On the open land to the left, two houses, 'West End' and 'Fieldheys', now stand. Apart from these and the rough surfacing of the road, little has changed in ninety years.

THATCHED COTTAGE, PEARCROFT ROAD. At least two Stonehouse postcard views exist of thatched cottages long since demolished. The first was at Hayward's End, roughly where the entrance to 'The Nook' is now. The second, a much less common picture, is of this cottage in Pearcroft Road. Both speak volumes about the low maintenance standards of vernacular architecture in Edwardian England.

ST CYR'S PARISH CHURCH. This postcard of a much-ivied St Cyr's parish church is an interesting one, with its groups of onlookers and some splendid Victorian artificial flower wreaths beneath their protective glass domes. The picture dates from around 1910.

ST CYR'S CHURCH INTERIOR. The chancel of St Cyr's church, decorated with flowers, appears commonly on postcards. What is curious, however, is that the photographer has chosen to paint over the east window, giving it the appearance of a tapestry.

THE CHOIR OF ST CYR'S PARISH CHURCH, STONEHOUSE, 1923. Back row, left to right: Bill Mapson (organ blower), Harry Smith, Frank Gwinnell, Tom Tocknell, J.W. Rowbotham, Jack Price, ? Gale, Jimmy Elmer, Sgt Maj Gardiner (verger). Second row: Gladys Shardlow, Bill Pollard, Roy Neal, Geo. Parker, A.H. Vowles; H.E. Hawker, ? Golding, Herbert Munn, Florence Rowbotham, Gracie Souls. Third row: Doris Hughes, Mrs Pollard, Mrs Neal, Mrs Bingle, Mr Blick (churchwarden), Archie Boucher (organist and choirmaster), Revd Leonard Dawson (vicar), Revd Thomas (curate), Mr Tanner (churchwarden), Miss Lettie Boucher, Mrs Gwinnell, Miss Creed, Mrs Barnard. Front row: George Joyner, -?-, Harry Crook, Leslie Hill, Eric Marchant, Fred Joyner, -?-, -?-, -?-, Claude Coates, Lionel Coates, Tom Edwards, Jack Hobbs, Stan Joyner.

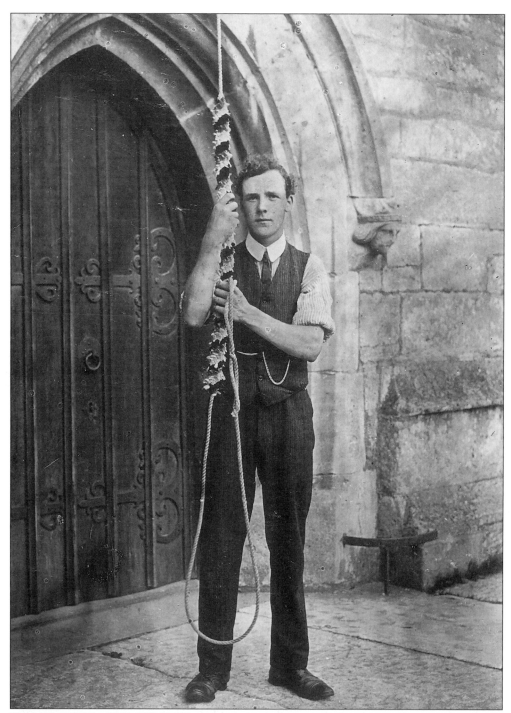

BELLRINGING, STONEHOUSE, *c.* 1910. Tom Price, who lived near the Royal Oak and whose father worked at the Brickworks, stands outside the west door of St Cyr's church. An external bell may have existed in this position, but it seems far more likely that the rope was just fixed to a bracket above for the purpose of achieving a well-lit photograph. Interestingly, the carved head to the right has eroded so as to be almost unrecognizable today.

FIRE AT STONEHOUSE COURT. In May 1908 a devastating fire occurred at Stonehouse Court. Discovered by postboy Vivian Stephens at 6.40a.m., the fire was already being tackled by two Stroud engines at 7 o'clock. (They had been summoned by telephone.) The house had only recently been renovated by its owner, Mr A.S. Winterbotham, who was on holiday at Westward Ho! Young Stephens had, it seems, run to the Police Station in the High Street in three minutes flat to report the blaze, which probably started in a smouldering kitchen fireplace beam and was fed by the gas system piped to almost every room. Loyal friends and parishioners saved most of the contents of the drawing room, including a grand piano, from the flames. An employee, John Richens, was badly injured by falling masonry and Captain P.H.R. Ford, in charge of one of the engines, had a lucky escape. Apparently, Wycliffe College in its entirety was permitted to come across to observe the destruction of the mansion.

BUILDING WORKERS, STONEHOUSE COURT. Here we see a group of craftsmen and labourers employed on the 1907 rebuilding of the Court, which took place only a year before the fire. They are standing at the main front entrance.

STONEHOUSE COURT INTERIOR. This photograph was bought at the sale of the contents of the Court in 1975, when Mrs Caroline Winterbotham died aged around 100. It shows the Hall, looking west, as it was after the 1907 refurbishment, but before the 1908 fire. Because it appeared like this for such a short time, it is clearly an important record of this brief period in the history of the building.

STONEHOUSE BRICK AND TILE COMPANY, c. 1907. The firm was founded in 1890, with Mr A.W. Anderson as its first manager. At one stage in its development it expanded into garden ornaments, offering a range of pigeons, squirrels, rabbits (large and small), frogs and mannikins at prices ranging from 1s 6d to 6s 6d.

The Wood
Doverow Hill.
669

DOVEROW HILL, c. 1907. Showing a footpath through the woods on Doverow Hill, this postcard is the work of E.P. Conway of Nailsworth and marks the extreme limit of the geographical area covered in his work.

CROWN AND ANCHOR HOTEL, *c.* 1890. The photographer of this interesting picture is not known, but it could well be P.L. Smith (1845-1932) who was working in Stonehouse at the time and later moved to Nailsworth.

CROWN AND ANCHOR HOTEL, *c.* 1905. By the time of this second view, by Frederick Restall, the central portion of the hotel has been rebuilt. Note the varied array of vehicles parked in front. The Midland Railway poster advertises excursions to destinations as far distant as Ilfracombe and the Isle of Man, together with information on a cheap-rate parcel service.

THE SPA INN, OLDENDS LANE. The Spa Inn, situated in Oldend Lane as it should perhaps be more correctly known, is structurally much the same today, though two porches and an extension have been added. Around 1910, when this photograph was taken, the inn sold Smith's Brimscombe Brewery Ales and its licensee was Charles Alder. Murray's Handbook of 1872 noted, 'There is a small pump-room over a spring of mineral water in the village', and C.L. Smith, a local historian, wrote that 'Gloucester coaches brought patients to Oldends as well as Bath; its waters were recommended as a stimulant, most useful in cases of palsy, rheumatism and gout.'

SEVERN VALLEY DAIRY PRODUCTS COMPANY. This building in the High Street, now known as Apsley House, was occupied around 1910 by the Severn Valley Dairy Products Company. It remains basically as shown in the photograph, though the gardens are much altered and the gas lamp has gone. Once owned by a Mr Bond, the firm was noted for the cheeses it produced.

STONEHOUSE CONGREGATIONAL CHURCH. Arguably one of Stonehouse's finer buildings, the Congregational Church founded in 1812 stood until 1967 in the High Street. A few of its gravestones still remain. Its early registers are at the Public Record Office in London.

CONGREGATIONAL CHURCH INTERIOR. The inside of the chapel follows the general design of countless nonconformist meeting houses.

ST CYR'S CHURCH HALL. Dating from between the wars, this picture shows not only a now much-altered structure, but also a dramatically different background, the result of subsequent development. The building was dedicated on 30 September 1933 and cost £1,658. A fire broke out in the Hall during the Second World War.

FAWKES' STORES. This is how the store appeared around 1905. Note the cluttered shop windows in front of which the staff are standing.

VERNEY RD STONEHOUSE 207

VERNEY ROAD. The principal differences between this 1930s postcard and the scene today is that the road has since been widened much further up and half a dozen more houses have been built to the left of the picture.

THE BATHING PLACE. Although sold by stationer Mark Whiley about 1915 as a postcard, this view of the River Frome, close to the point where the Midland Railway viaduct crosses it, dates in fact from around 1900. It was taken by W.A. Sibly of Wycliffe College 'in dim days in the distance enchanted, when I was young' as he rather quaintly put it.

DREDGING GANG AT WORK. This fine picture appears to show navvies working on an unidentified water course, probably part of the Stroudwater Canal. It is by H. Lockyer of Stonehouse, so may be assumed to be somewhere within, or close to, the parish.

PRICE'S NURSERIES, RYEFORD. John Price and Sons Ltd, Nurserymen, Seedsmen and Florists, had extensive premises at Ryeford. Their advertisements claimed they had 'one of the finest collections of exotic flowering plants in the county'. There was another branch of the business at Kings Stanley. The Ryeford site is now occupied by Kennedy's Garden Centre.

HORSE-DRAWN TIMBER WAGON. This fine, though damaged, photograph is endorsed with the message 'Stonehouse Brushworks, 1913'. The date would seem accurate, but it is far more likely, from the size of the wagon and the team of six draught horses, that it in fact relates to Ryeford Sawmills.

HAULAGE VEHICLE. Sentinel steam lorries, made at Shrewsbury, enjoyed a wide distribution. They were popular from around 1920 to 1935, though a few were made after the Second World War, when a consignment of a hundred or so was sent to Argentina. The company also had a plant at Liverpool. This vehicle, intended for R.W. Baker of Stonehouse, was probably photographed near the factory rather than locally.

GWR STATION, STONEHOUSE. One of Stonehouse stationer G.W. Timbrell's series of postcards, this 1920s picture shows a train arriving from Gloucester. To the far left, the railcar stands at the opposite platform.

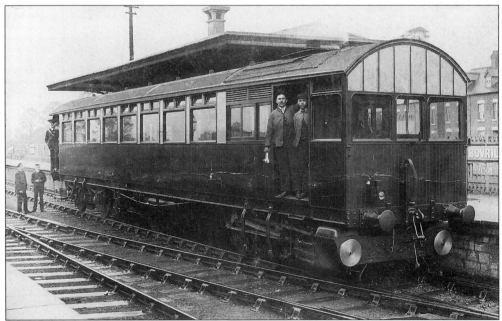

THE GWR RAILCAR. This much earlier photograph dates from 1903, the period of the inception of the service. The crew are seen aboard one of their newly acquired railcars.

STONEHOUSE MIDLAND RAILWAY STATION, *c.* 1920. Passengers are about to board the Bristol train just arriving from Gloucester. A notice board advises travellers to change here for Stroud and the Nailsworth branch.

MIDLAND RAILWAY LANDSLIP, STONEHOUSE. As far as Mr Fred Rowbotham can recall, this mishap took place around 1912 or 1913 and involved the collapse of a portion of the railway viaduct carrying the line between The Ocean and Beard's Mill. It was apparently audible in Eastington and caused a blockage of the stream which flows near the site of the accident.

HAYWARD'S END. Dating from the early or mid-seventeenth century, when it was in the possession of the Fowler family, Hayward's End takes its name from later owners. By 1910, when the photograph was taken, Mr Edward Jenner Davies was in residence.

THE HAYWARD FAMILY. These carte-de-visite sized studies are of Martinus Peter Hayward (1817-1904) and Mary his wife (1834-1879). The photographs, both carefully hand-tinted, are good examples of Victorian portraiture of the 1860s or 1870s. The Haywards' daughter, Helen Elizabeth (1858-1943), married Edward Jenner Davies (1851-1926), who lived at Hayward's End during the first quarter of the present century.

MISS C.M. JENNER DAVIES. Miss Jenner Davies, daughter of Edward and Helen Elizabeth, was an able and talented lady. She was, for instance, responsible for the compilation of the photographic album from which this picture is taken, involved herself with early motor vehicles, travelled widely and, at one stage, ran a cricket eleven (see page 7)!

THE JENNER DAVIES FAMILY'S HORSES. In the yard leading from Hayward's End onto Bath Road, grooms Fred and (right) William pose with Orby, Kama, Komet and Sammy. The photograph dates from around 1910.

THE SIBLY FAMILY, *c.* 1891. G.W. Sibly (seated) founded Wycliffe College in 1882 and was its first headmaster. He is seen here, a decade or so later, with his wife and children. Behind stand his brother F.A. Sibly and sister-in-law Florence.

WYCLIFFE COLLEGE CYCLISTS, *c.* 1884. In this important but somewhat faded photograph, a splendid array of penny-farthings (plus one slightly more modern-looking machine) is shown off by an enthusiastic group of young students. The picture dates from only a couple of years after the foundation of the College.

WATER SPORTS AT WYCLIFFE COLLEGE. In 1905 the Stroudwater Canal and College Boathouse (which still survives) were the scene for either a rowing or a swimming competition. Note the somewhat primitive hut by the water's edge and the inquisitive youngster who has climbed up onto it to enjoy a better view of the proceedings.

SWIMMING SPORTS, 1905. Taken the same year as the picture above, this photograph shows an exciting stage in the obstacle race. A competitor is wading ashore, having just descended the slide, which is being re-watered, whilst D.G. Lewis and Horace Jones negotiate the five-barred gate.

SUFFERING STUDENTS. This amusing, if slightly pathetic, picture of Wycliffe College pupils dates from around 1900 and needs no further explanation other than its original caption: 'Three little boys with the mumps!'

FIRE AT WYCLIFE COLLEGE CHAPEL. A disastrous fire broke out in the chapel on 21 November 1939. The building was gutted and all its woodwork and internal fitments were destroyed. A press report described the fine organ as 'disappearing completely'. Fire crews from Stonehouse and Stroud were, however, able to save the tower, where the clock, it was noted, marked the height of the battle by stopping at 1.20p.m. Erected originally in 1911, the chapel was rebuilt after the war and still serves the College.

WOODWORK CLASS, WYCLIFFE COLLEGE. This postcard, one of a large series by P.A. Buchanan and Co. of Croydon, though very obviously posed, gives a fair idea of the facilities for woodwork which the College possessed around 1910.

SCHOOL HOUSE DINING ROOM, WYCLIFFE COLLEGE. Part of the same series as the last illustration, this postcard allows an insight into the domestic life of College pupils during Edwardian days. Note the mixture of benches and chairs and the small table on the dais between the windows, presumably to allow the duty master an elevated position from which to inspect the eating habits of his charges. Also of interest are the funnel-like fume extraction ducts above the gas lamps set into the walls.

THE GARDENS, WYCLIFFE COLLEGE. This photograph, probably taken by W.A. Sibly around 1900, reveals the layout of flower beds and the position of urns and greenhouses. More significantly perhaps, it shows what must surely be the earliest picture of the local recording of weather data, for which the College has become so justly renowned over the years.

WINDRUSH, WYCLIFFE JUNIOR SCHOOL. In this pleasantly relaxed 1940s scene, young pupils play cricket in front of 'Windrush', one of the Junior School boarding houses.

QUEEN VICTORIA'S GOLDEN JUBILEE, STONEHOUSE. One of an important late nineteenth century series of photographs of which Stonehouse can be justly proud, this records the 1887 decorations on the Green. The Globe Inn and its associated buildings are visible in the background. Contemporary reports also describe other decorations and relate the events of this special day. There were arches at Hayward's End and at the entrance to the Vicarage Grounds. 'Venetian masts', with shields, flags and streamers, were placed at the top of Regent Street. Another large banner decked the entrance to the GWR station. In the evening there was an illuminated crown above the doorway of the Institute. Celebrations during the day included hoisting the royal standard, singing the Jubilee Anthem, distributing medals, a free dinner for 950 people, a band, a free tea, sports, entertainments, rockets and a beacon on Doverow Hill.

QUEEN VICTORIA'S DIAMOND JUBILEE CELEBRATIONS. A fitting companion to the last picture, this view shows a similar scene ten years later in 1897 and is taken from the opposite side of the Green. The gap between the buildings leads into what is now Quietways. The War Memorial currently occupies the approximate site of the decorated table. The celebrations were much as in 1887, though this time between 1,400 and 1,500 sat down to tea! At 6p.m., it was recorded, Mr Jenner Davies returned to Stonehouse from London, having actually seen the Queen in her procession through the capital.

STONEHOUSE SCHOOLBOYS. This is the boys' playground of the old primary school in Elm Road. Since there are cricket bats and wickets in evidence it must be a summer picture.It dates from around 1910. The writer of the postcard, George Partridge, is sending it to say thank you for his birthday presents, 'a cake, a ball and a sixpence'.

LAYING THE FOUNDATION STONE, STONEHOUSE BAPTIST CHURCH HALL. The ceremony captured here by photographer Frederick Restall depicts one of the four foundation stones of the Baptist Church Hall off Queen's Road being laid on 29 January 1908. The building, intended to seat 250, is now the Top Cue Sports and Social Club. The original idea was for the existing structure to serve only as a hall, since a church was to be built where the garages now stand.

CORONATION BONFIRE, STONEHOUSE, 1911. Celebrations at Stonehouse for the Coronation of King George V in June 1911 included several church services, flag raising and singing the National Anthem on the parish church tower, two sports programmes (children in the afternoon and adults in the evening) and, of course, the lighting of the Coronation bonfire. Amongst the crowd in front of it, identified by an object protruding from his pocket, is Ted White who, now nearly 97 years old, remembers so much about Edwardian Stonehouse and, blessed with good eyesight and an excellent memory, is a charming, humorous and informative raconteur.

PRESENTATION OF HORSE TROUGH AT RYEFORD. The presentation took place in September 1914. The trough was given by the Stonehouse Band of Mercy and received on behalf of the Parish Council by Chairman Mr J. Westacott. The Press commented 'there was no doubt that it was a great acquisition and already it had been used a great deal.'

STONEHOUSE FLOWER SHOW, 1907, COMIC FOOTBALL MATCH. A record number of horticultural entries was noted in the *Stroud News* write-up of the Flower Show, though 'there was a fall off in honey, probably on account of the cold and wet weather which caused the bees to become less active than usual'. However, for the Village Sports which accompanied the festivities there was wholly unqualified praise. Events included a costume-changing race, a 100 yards football race, and slow bicycle and blindfold races. The comic football match was the sparkling finale. The upper picture shows the participants lined up ready to commence play; the lower one the four entries judged to have the best fancy dress: they appear to be standing in order of merit from right to left.

MID-GLOUCESTERSHIRE HISTORICAL PAGEANT OF PROGRESS, 1911. Acted out at Fromehall Park, Stroud, by a thousand people from all around the area, this was possibly the greatest theatrical spectacle the district has ever seen. Stonehouse, Eastington and the Stanleys were responsible for the opening episode, entitled 'Britons and Romans'. In the first of this pair of photographs we see the conquering imperial legions of Rome; in the second, the native people they overcame.

TAKING TEDDY FOR A RIDE. This charming study of an unnamed young lady, thought possibly to be a member of the Carter or Taylor families, is by the Stonehouse photographer H. Lockyer. A doll and what appears to be a new teddy bear are shown off proudly to the camera, whilst a recumbent canine observer looks on warily.

OPENING OF THE NEW POST OFFICE, STONEHOUSE, NOVEMBER 1933. The new post office at Stonehouse, built entirely of local bricks, was actually opened by Sir Stephen Tallents, Public Relations Officer of the GPO. However, the limelight on this occasion was surely stolen by Lady Beatrice Marling, who went behind the counter and sold the first stamp to local MP Mr Robert Perkins. This photograph comes from the Marling family's private collection.

SILVER JUBILEE CARNIVAL, 1935. This picture is reputed to show the 1935 Silver Jubilee Carnival, with entrants standing in front of the Crown and Anchor Hotel. The events of the day had begun with their meeting up at the bottom of Woodcock Lane. Judging was by Sir John Palmer (probably the blurred figure in the trilby) on the Green. The procession, led by the May Queen, Joan Summers, then set off for the Recreation Field. Later came a Punch and Judy Show, sports (junior and adult) and, as dusk fell, a torchlight procession, followed by fireworks and the lighting of the Jubilee Bonfire on Doverow Hill. Notice the large pig to the right of the picture.

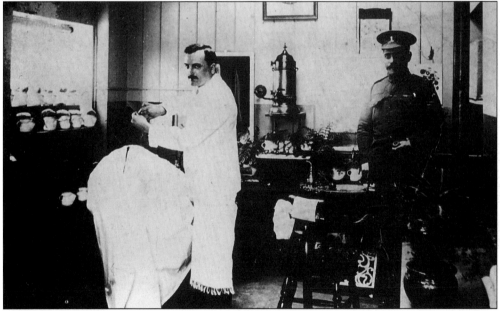

BARBER'S SHOP INTERIOR. In this unusual photograph Mr Taylor is seen in his barber's shop on the north side of Bath Road, near the junction with Regent Street. On the right is Sgt. Maj. Gardiner. This celebrated local hero was wounded in action in October 1914, being mentioned in despatches. *The Times* of 5 November 1914 reported that, 'The Medaille Militaire, France's highest military award, has been bestowed on Sgt. Maj. Gardiner, 11th Hussars, for gallantry during operations between August 21st and 30th 1914.'

COMIC CARNIVAL ENTRY. Here Mr Edwards, a renowned character and practical joker, is seen entering a local carnival. I have been unable to discover how the cow responded to the whip. Accompanying him is his wife.

ALBERT AND LOUISA WITTS. In this peaceful photograph, which dates from around the 1930s, Mr and Mrs Witts sit in the garden of their cottage in the meadows behind Stonehouse Brushworks.

PUSHBALL MATCH, STONEHOUSE FLOWER SHOW, 1906. Dr J. McLannahan's organizing committee for the 1906 Stonehouse Horticultural Society's Annual Flower Show, held on Laburnum Walk Field, was well pleased with the standard of entries. Mr J. Shore, Lord Fitzhardinge's gardener and one of the judges, considered it 'the best show in the history of the society'. The general opinion of the viewing public too, according to the *Stroud News*, was that 'there was absolutely no rubbish to be detected by the assiduously quizzical'. The committee was also pleased that it had come up with an unusual spectator sport to occupy the crowds: American pushball. In the lower picture the ball is seen held aloft at one end of the field. In the upper, a competition is under way. Alf Carter, the writer of the postcard on which this latter view appears, informs us that it is Joe Price's team versus the Brickyard and adds (a trifle sadly) 'but you cannot see me as I am the other side of the ball'.

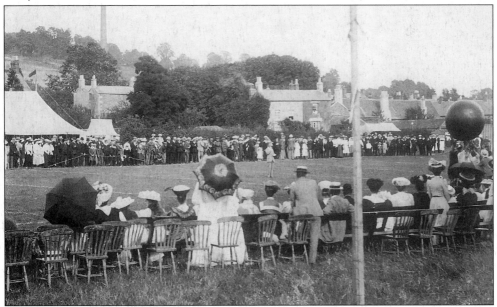

STONEHOUSE PRIMITIVE METHODIST CHAPEL, *c.* 1900. This iron building, put up first at Ryeford around 1870, was re-erected a couple of decades later in Regent Street, where it served as a Methodist Meeting House until superseded in 1911 by the present Wycliffe College Chapel in Bath Road.

A SEVERN TROW UNLOADING, *c.* 1915. Photographs of working vessels on the Stroudwater Canal are relatively uncommon, which accounts for the importance of this picture of a trow at Ryeford Sawmills Wharf. Note the partitioning boards in the hold and the canvas sidesheets; also the juxtaposition of a working boat with a Wycliffe College pleasure craft.

Two
Kings Stanley

HARVESTING NEAR MIDDLEYARD. No pictorial study of Kings Stanley would be complete without this superb rural photograph. In the middle distance stands the Baptist Chapel, with its manse to the left and schoolroom built on to the right.

Although in the Middle Ages the Stanleys were of similar size and importance, by 1900 Kings Stanley had a population of some 1,150 and was half as large again as its neighbour. This may in part be explained by employment opportunities: Stanley Mill offered work to several hundred, while the proximity of Ryeford station permitted easier access to jobs in the central Stroud area.

Jeptha Young, the Kings Stanley poet, writing in 1880, commented:

From Selsley's high and noted hill,
You have a view of Stanley Mill
Where woollen cloths are made
Of almost every name and hue,
As black, or brown, or green, or blue,
Broad, double-milled and tweed.

The mill, built in the early nineteenth century, has an iron-framed interior structure of national architectural importance.

Kings Stanley is a parish with a long and varied history and both Roman and Medieval sites within its boundaries have, in recent years, been excavated. From the former period survive stone altars, discovered in Victorian times, and a stamped tile from the factory of Arverius.

Many fine buildings remain within the parish – for instance Stanley House, Borough Farm, The Rectory and Beech House. In the churchyard are preserved several unusual memorials. One records the untimely death in 1804 of eight-year-old Martha Collins, a publican's daughter, who drowned after falling into a barrel of beer:

'Twas as she tript from cask to cask
In at a bung hole quickly fell.
Suffocation was her task,
She had not time to say farewell.

Another records the murder in 1830 of a member of the Wilkins family who met his death, as his tombstone states, from 'a stab of a knife by the hand of John Dangerfield his nephew'.

Nonconformity came particularly early to Kings Stanley. A Baptist Chapel at Middleyard, still flourishing, is said to have been founded in 1640. In more recent times and on a lighter note, a certain Miss Dallimore, who taught in the Sunday School there, owned a parrot which had been taught to sing 'Praise my soul the King of Heaven'! There was also a Primitive Methodist Chapel. Amongst many other village institutions was the Kings Stanley Band, which still exists and which performed in a splendid blue uniform with red and silver facings.

MIDDLEYARD. From the right, the road from Selsley leads down into Middleyard. The back of the Baptist Chapel can be seen. This photograph was taken in summer, around 1910.

VILLAGE BOYS, MIDDLEYARD. In this evocative turn-of-the-century scene, village boys chat in the road in front of the Baptist Chapel, while a cyclist pauses to watch the photographer. The youngster on the left may be a delivery boy, or is perhaps just on an errand for his mother.

KINGS STANLEY BAPTIST AFC. The season is 1931-2 and the team are, back row: R. Cave, -?-, R. Arnold, S. Cole, R. King, J. Griffiths, H. Kent, Revd Mason. Front row: J. Kirby, R. Capener, L. Baker, J. Gale, S. Cook, E. Wheeler.

KINGS STANLEY BAPTIST BIBLE CLASS, 1911. Nonconformist Bible classes at this period were often single sex organizations and it is fair to assume there may well have been a parallel meeting for men. Note the splendid array of Sunday hats. The photograph is by Henry Comley of Stroud.

CARNIVAL, MIDDLEYARD, *c.* 1950. The participants in the Middleyard Baptist Chapel Carnival shown in this delightful photograph are, left to right: Linda Smith, Alan Gale, Gillian Allen, Thelma Franklin (?), Ruth Gale (?), Wendy Bramwich, Jennifer Cook, Peter Cook, -?-, Michael Bale, Patricia Bale.

CO-OPERATIVE SOCIETY'S PREMISES. This early 1920s picture of the Cainscross and Ebley Co-operative Society's number 5 branch in New Street, Kings Stanley, has manager Sid Chandler between two assistants. He later left the firm and set up his own business in a corrugated iron building opposite, now the fish and chip shop.

BROAD STREET, *c.* 1910. Ladies with prams and small children would be ill advised to linger in the road in Broad Street today. The chapel on the left was of the Primitive Methodist persuasion and was built in 1861. It has recently seen service as, successively, an antique shop and a guest house.

BATH ROAD. In this postcard of around 1910 scaffolding has been put up for the building of Bath Villa, the final house in the row. A brick pile by the roadside announces that work is beginning. The perry orchard on the left has given way to residential development.

OLD COTTAGES, WOODSIDE LANE. This slightly damaged picture shows the old cottages in Woodside Lane which were demolished in the 1950s. The card was posted in 1919 but could well have been taken a full decade earlier.

WOODSIDE RACE. This highly unusual inter-war years annual Easter event is still remembered by the older residents of Kings Stanley. Woodside Race was the result of half-friendly rivalry between Harry Bailey (left) and Bill Ecott and appears to have been conceived while the two were drinking together in their local hostelry. The course selected was Woodside Lane, which is where the competitors (who were, it must be said, already past the first flush of youth) are pictured, raring to go. Also shown are, left to right, Jack Stockwell, Jack French, Roy Malpas, 'Pop' Malpas and Dennis Adams.

THE UPPER GREEN, *c.* 1907. This view must date from only a year or so before the erection of the pump and is taken from the opposite direction to the picture below. Note Liddiatt's Cycle Depot (back left) and, on the right, the inn sign for the Crown, which was served by Godsell's Brewery of Stroud. On the reverse is an amusing message reporting that 'we put Owen in the baby show at Stonehouse. He came off with flying colours. All the gentry was gone on Owen. They were pleased with his black eyes!'

THE UPPER GREEN. In this view Kingston House is on the right. The parish pump dominates the central area of the picture and, beyond it, the High Street disappears off towards the King's Head. It would be interesting to discover who published the extensive series of postcards, of which this is one, which appeared in the 1920s and 1930s and carried a four figure serial number.

THE OLD CROWN, *c.* 1910. The public house (left) is an early building, with portions possibly dating back as far as the fifteenth century. The old village workhouse was formerly located in the complex beyond the inn sign. The photograph is brought to life by the crowd of village children, several with iron hoops.

THE KING'S HEAD. This Edwardian picture shows the King's Head without its dormers, of which it acquired first two, then four. The red brick building on the right is the old post office. The road surface is clearly unmetalled and chickens roam free on the Green, where a Whitsun fair continued to be held within living memory.

THE WAR MEMORIAL. On Saturday 9 October 1920 Kings Stanley's War Memorial was officially dedicated by Lady Marling. A special card was issued by the local football club, commemorating W.R. Bishop, T. Bassett, A. Collins, E.A.G. Gabb and W.G. Rodway 'who died whilst engaged in the greatest game of all'. The ball-shaped wreath is the club's floral tribute. Postcards were also produced in remembrance of at least two of those who died. His brother is said to have seen Private Gabb for the last time, being carried wounded off the beach at Suvla Bay, Gallipoli. Insets: E.A.G. Gabb (left) and W.G. Rodway.

HOLLEY'S SHOP, *c.* 1935. Holley Bros' grocery and provisions store is on the right, with Miss James about to leave through the gateway. School House is seen on the left side of Church Street.

HOLLEY'S SHOP FRONT, *c.* 1935. In the doorway of their shop stand brothers Ewart (left) and Francis Holley. Note the unusual enamelled advertisement plaque to the left of the door.

VILLAGE PARADE. This picture is thought to show troop recruitment in 1914 at Kings Stanley. The parade is led by the scouts. In the background is the village band.

MILITARY PARADE. Now in uniform, recruits parade in front of the King's Head, ironically on the same spot where the memorial to many of them would later be erected. Holley's shop is on the left.

THE OLD BAKERY. This business occupied the building onto which 'Images' hair styling shop in the High Street is now built. It has been much altered. Note the advertisement panels. At different periods, shops in various parts of this ancient edifice have sold both sweets and cycles.

CHURCH STREET, c. 1908. The King's Head (far right) appears frequently on early postcards of Kings Stanley. The New Inn, however, was rarely photographed. Next to it is a small shop where, in the 1950s, Mrs Estop sold sweets. Beyond, in the middle distance, may be seen the greenhouses of John Price and Son Ltd, whose headquarters were at Ryeford (see page 25).

KINGS STANLEY BRITISH LEGION. On 10 October 1948 the women's section standard of the Kings Stanley Branch of the British Legion was dedicated. The photograph shows the procession on its way to the church. The balding gentleman walking behind the bass drummer is thought to be local MP Robert Perkins.

RECTORY FIELD. In the 1920s parish events were often held here. Flags festoon the Rectory itself in this picture, and discernible at an upstairs window is a banner bearing the arms of Jesus College Cambridge, patron of the living of Kings Stanley.

KINGS STANLEY GARAGE, c. 1930. George Parkin, seen here with his wife in the doorway of the garage, was a well-known and popular village character. He hit the headlines, two years before his death in 1989 a month short of his century, as the oldest competitor in the West of England conker championships held on the village green. Under the terms of his will groceries to the value of £10 each were to be distributed to 100 old folk in the village. In the second picture, taken in the 1950s, the shell of the new garage building has been erected over the original one.

THE AVENUE. Of this pair of Edwardian views, the first looks down the Avenue towards the church. The end building was, for many years, a shop. The second, clearly taken on a windy day, faces up towards the village centre and was taken just in front of the church gates. The scene is unrecognizable today.

ST GEORGE'S AVENUE, *c.* 1940. By the end of the 1930s the Avenue had been transformed by housing development – private on the right, council on the left. The author's grandfather's building firm, W.E. Beard and Son of Stroud, erected the latter.

KINGS STANLEY CHURCH. This is thought to be one of the earliest surviving photographs of the parish, dating from around 1870. Note the two sets of external steps leading to the nave gallery, long since demolished.

KINGS STANLEY CHURCH CHOIR, 1928-1929. Back row, left to right: H. Liddiatt, W. Pollard, L. Wall (crucifer), F. Gleed, M. Camm. Second row: N. Moss, D. Tocknell, I. Tocknell, M. Taylor, I. Ireland, G. Chandler, E. Elliott, V. Chandler, E. Chandler. Third row: D. Vines, W. Garnes, J. Vaile, E. Gleed, Revd Jennings, Revd Layng, W.E. James (organist and choirmaster), A. Harrison, M. Harrison, D. Richardson. Seated on the ground: H. Blick, H. Slyman, J. Chandler, T. Wall, D. Wall, R. Frith.

CONSECRATION OF THE NEW AREA OF THE CHURCHYARD. This photograph is of the then Bishop of Gloucester at Kings Stanley around 1920, dedicating the new section of the graveyard near the church gates.

STANLEY HOUSE. A postcard view of this early building, photographed from further to the right, full on with the middle gable, is quite common. This splendid view of the magnificent conservatory is not. Note also the bellcote.

'JEAN.' Jean seems to have belonged to the family of Marcus Cartwright, JP, of Beech House. Whether she enjoyed dressing up to have her photograph taken is uncertain.

STANLEY MILL. Dating from 1860, this early engraving shows the west facade of the celebrated mill, Stanley House and the church. In the foreground a rustic bridge crosses the Stroudwater Canal.

STANLEY MILL, c. 1890. Seen from across the mill reservoir, Stanley Mill looks structurally much the same today, more than a century on, though the cottages far left have gone and those to the right of the washing line are now derelict. The photograph is by either Paul Smith (1845-1932) or his brother Oliver.

MILLWORKERS. On the right is Elsie Ireland (née Tocknell) of Kings Stanley. The location is probably not this parish and could be either Bond's Mill at Stonehouse, or Apperly's Mill at Dudbridge, but the picture is too important to omit. The rosettes are thought to date it to 1910, when two general elections took place, one in January and one in December.

MILLWORKERS, STANLEY MILL. King George V's Silver Jubilee in 1935 was evidently marked with considerable festivities at Stanley Mill. Behind the left flag is Harry Gough. Most of the men in the front row were loom-tuners. Employees of Stanley Mill were brought to work by lorry from as far afield as Chalford.

THE SWEEPS V. THE MILLERS. We have a precise date for this event: 16 September 1911. It was one of many such comic football matches (see page 40). However, this particular event appears to have been ignored by the local press, so no background information is available. The theme, however, is obvious and the black and white costumes and make-up contrast splendidly. In the centre, wearing a white topper, is W. Ireland.

KINGS STANLEY FOOTBALL TEAM, *c.* 1920. This team has come down to us complete with some wonderful nicknames. Back row: W. Ireland, F. Gale, H. Howell, A. Loveday, G. Howell. Middle row: M. Dangerfield, E. 'Chilly' Malpas, 'Chappie' Price. Front row: W. Pearce, A. Elliott, B. Edmonds, W. Flight, J. Franklin. Recumbent: 'Shoddy' Stockwell.

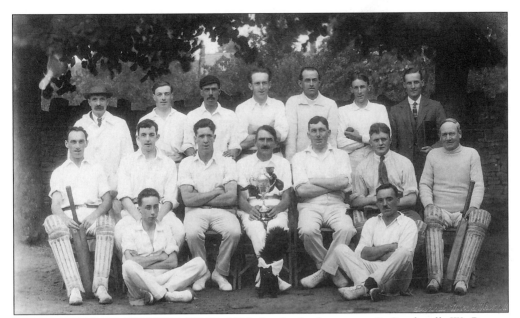

KINGS STANLEY CRICKET CLUB, 1925. In the back row are S. Stockwell, W. Pearce, J. Cave, S. Chandler, J. Lawrence, W. Ireland, M. Ellis. Middle row: H. Howell, J.F. Stockwell, W. Gale, J. Griffiths, A. Stockwell, J. Blanch, A.E. Stafford. Front row, seated on the ground: A. Elliott, C.A. Brown.

KINGS STANLEY SCOUTS. This appears to show either the local scouts attempting to construct a shelter with wheat straw over canvas, or a rural skills competition in thatching.

THE LIBERAL PARTY COMMITTEE. Taken, it is thought, at the Council School at the entrance to Peck Street, this is believed to show the Kings Stanley Liberal Party Committee at the time of the 1918 December general election. Third and fourth from the right are Mr Gabb and W. Ireland respectively.

MILK DELIVERY. By 1920 Spratts of Kings Stanley no longer ran their horse bus. Instead, they now concentrated on more up-to-date commercial forms of transport. Here a Model T Ford is seen at Coaley loaded with $17\frac{1}{2}$ gallon milk churns intended for delivery to Cadbury's chocolate factory at Frampton-on-Severn. The driver is Leslie Mayo.

BREAD DELIVERY. Miss Gertrude Champion, later Mrs Leslie Mayo, sets out on her rounds accompanied, as usual, by her dog. She often carried two baskets, one fixed on behind. The photograph was taken around 1920.

A MOCK WEDDING AT KINGS STANLEY. This event was staged during the last war to raise funds for village servicemen, the idea being that all attending the 'reception' in the old Pavilion should make a contribution. Food was donated and children, so one youngster of the time remembers, were not allowed in the building. Those pictured are (left to right) Jack French, Stan Chandler, Mrs French, Fred Franklin, Walter Abel, Gladys Daniels and Mr Melhuish.

RYEFORD SAWMILLS, *c.* 1890. Though strictly speaking in Stonehouse parish, this early photograph is included here because it is thought to show Kings Stanley people: two generations of the Tocknell family are known to be present, though they have not been precisely identified. The taller boy is Frank Flight. The picture is arguably one of the most important in this collection since it records both employees in their work clothes and, more significantly, the tools and machinery used at the sawmill.

Opposite: PEACE CELEBRATIONS, 1945. Celebrations to commemorate the end of World War Two included a concert in the Pavilion. A youthful Jill Griffin is seated to the left of Britannia's shield, with Judy Adams to the right. Britannia herself is Margaret Fletcher.

JOHN BRINKWORTH, HEDGER AND DITCHER. Datable to around 1880, this splendid portrait depicts the workaday habit of a labourer employed in what was then a vital rural occupation.

Three
Leonard Stanley

HAY HARVEST, LEONARD STANLEY. This delightfully composed photograph of around 1908 looks across Seven Waters towards St Swithin's church beyond the trees in the middle distance.

Leonard Stanley is a most attractive village, built predominantly in local stone, though with some brick and a little half-timbering. The original dedication of the church was to St Leonard, but this was later altered to St Swithin. It once formed part of an Augustinian (later Benedictine) priory of which some interesting buildings remain.

In medieval times Leonard Stanley held weekly markets and was a relatively important parish. From this period The Mercer's House survives, with deeds dating back to the fourteenth century. Another fine house, The Grange, was built in 1580, while The Priory, adjoining the church and partly on the site of the domestic buildings of its medieval namesake, was rebuilt with a fine classical facade in the mid-eighteenth century.

In 1686 Leonard Stanley, which then contained many fine half-timbered buildings, suffered a major fire, as a result of which a Royal Brief was issued, intended for circulation throughout the South West of England. Its purpose was to collect alms for Leonard Stanley's stricken inhabitants. As this document, quaintly punctuated, states, 'Upon Wednesday the Three and Twentieth day of March last past, between the hours of One and Two in the Afternoon of the same day, there happened a Sudden and Lamentable Fire in the Market Town of Leonard Stanley … which within the space of Three hours consumed to Ashes and burnt down to the Ground … houses consisting of One Hundred and Four bays of building … amounting to the sum of Three Thousand and Seven Hundred Pounds, and upwards.' Nineteen families were left homeless. When rebuilding took place it was largely in more durable Cotswold stone, which of course has resulted in the central area of the village looking as it does today.

By 1910, when some of the photographs in this chapter were taken, the Wesleyan Chapel (founded a century earlier) was flourishing, a post office was in existence and the population was around 700. Jeptha Young, of Kings Stanley, composed an amusing poem in which he fancied that the newly-restored church clock addressed the people of the parish:

Near twenty years I idle stood,
Though time was flying quick,
My hammer never gave a stroke,
Nor pendulum a tick.
But now, though it should rain or shine,
My duty shall be done,
And every day at dinner time
I'll sound out number One.

Then for an hour you know full well
You have no work to do
Until I strike the tenor bell
And sound out number Two.

The poem continues in like vein through to twelve o'clock.

ST SWITHIN'S CHURCH INTERIOR. So much has changed since this Edwardian postcard was made that even regular churchgoers might have to look twice to recognize the building. The west gallery has disappeared, along with the box pews, lights have gone, the ceiling vault is altered and the pulpit has been replaced. All these differences, of course, point up why the photograph constitutes such an important historical document.

ST SWITHIN'S CHURCH RESTORATION. In this picture, dating from between the wars, major structural repairs are being undertaken at St Swithin's. The large and rather ominous crack above the chancel arch suggests why such work was necessary.

CHURCH ROAD IN WINTER. This charming snow scene of around 1911 was, not surprisingly perhaps, overprinted 'Season's Greetings'.

CHURCH ROAD IN SUMMER. Taken at a different time of year, and a generation or so later, this second picture is believed to show the local Co-operative Society bread delivery van.

PRIORY FARM POOL. A beautifully composed scene, with tree silhouettes and reflections, this view of some of the old monastic buildings has in fact changed little since the late twenties when it was taken. At around this period Mrs Margaret Thomas recalls being taken as a child to see the ancient and decrepit 'Domesday Oak' which then still stood within the farm grounds.

VIEW FROM THE CHURCH TOWER. Dating from *c.* 1907, this well-known picture shows much of the main street of Leonard Stanley, including the Methodist Chapel which was founded in 1808 and has now been converted into a private house.

VIEW TOWARDS THE VICARAGE. In this second photograph, taken *c.* 1930 from the same vantage point as the last, we see the early cottages which face the graveyard and, to the right, the ivied facade of the vicarage.

THE STREET AND THE WAR MEMORIAL. At around the same period, another group of children pose by the War Memorial for photographer William Adams. Several subsequent alterations can be observed to the buildings: the large door in the White Hart, for instance, is now a window.

THE OLD POST OFFICE. The old post office in Bath Road, seen beyond the group of children, is now a private house. This photograph, which dates from around 1914, shows, left to right, front row, Cyril Minett, Doris Cook, Mabel Cook, Lily Pearce, Nancy Pearce and Ivy Pearce. The three children standing just behind them are William Fowler, Laura Cook and Ewart Smith.

THE MARSH. Around 1909 some fine specimens of topiary were to be found in the garden of what is now Yew Tree Cottage. Further down the road demolition has taken place. The plaque on the wall advertises the premises of G.W. Gardner, Baker and Grocer.

SEVEN WATERS. This is a peaceful village study, with a horse and trap in the distance. Harris' general stores are in the foreground. The photograph dates from around the period of the First World War. The shop has been rebuilt further back from the road. Some old cottages beyond have been replaced by new properties.

VICARAGE COTTAGE. This photograph records a most attractive cottage which once stood in Marsh Road but has entirely disappeared.

THE STREET, LOOKING NORTH. Interesting for reasons of costume and social life, this picture of The Street is full of action and detail. The couple on the left have been identified as Mr and Mrs Lewis. Note, in the middle distance, the tall chimney of Wothers' bakery. As with so many Leonard Stanley photographs, naming of villagers has been possible thanks to the excellent memory of Mrs Doris Hale.

THE STREET, LOOKING SOUTH. Here, in this companion picture, groups of villagers look on curiously while the photographer sets up his tripod. Note the two (rather overgrown) occupants of the pram and the dilapidated state of the exposed half-timbering on the right. For students of costume this also is a most interesting scene.

POWELL'S SHOP. Opposite the church was Samuel Powell's shop, now a private house. The board on the wall proudly announced that he was a grocer, baker, confectioner and china and earthenware dealer. It is recalled that the shop was run for many years by Samuel's daughter who sold, amongst other things, butter from Priory Farm.

BEARD'S MILL. Beard's Mill lies at the far extremity of Leonard Stanley parish, near its border with Stonehouse. This Edwardian view is by Frederick Restall. From the 1660s members of the Beard family are recorded as renting the mill, which they bought during the following century. In 1821 a 14 hp beam engine was installed. The mill passed out of the ownership of the Beard family in the mid-nineteenth century.

BONFIRE GROUP, GEORGE V'S CORONATION. Here we see the men responsible for Leonard Stanley's 1911 Coronation bonfire, presumably setting out for The Knoll where, as the next picture shows, they were once more photographed. Points of interest in this superb picture include the horse, with its straw boater, the array of axes and cleavers with which the party has armed itself, and the teddy bear mascot tied to the flagpole.

CORONATION BONFIRE, THE KNOLL, JUNE 1911. This is a splendid and justly celebrated photograph. The day's festivities began with a peal of bells. This was followed by the singing of the National Anthem on the church tower. A procession followed at 10a.m., with a fancy-dress competition and maypole dancing. A lunch for 500 in the long barn at The Priory followed at 1.15p.m., tea at 4p.m., with mugs and medals for the children, then finally the bonfire in the late evening, lit by Mrs Bonsey. The men second and third from the top of the ladder are Ernest Powell and George Smith respectively. The group at ground level includes Arthur Clark, William Pearce, Howard Powell and Fred Stafford.

COTTAGE, THE KNOLL. This attractive house, with extensions now built onto both sides, still enjoys its peaceful and secluded position at the far end of Gypsy Lane. The photographer, Lockyer, is remembered as living in a cottage, now demolished, which stood in a neighbouring field.

THE TANNERY, SEVEN WATERS. Stephen Mills' in-depth study of this important industrial complex, demolished some five years ago, makes it clear that Leonard Stanley tannery was one of the last surviving water-powered tanneries in the county. Its operational period was roughly a century beginning in the 1840s, during which time it was run in turn by three families, the Bryants, Tileys and Kitchens. The buildings shown nearest to camera in this photograph by John Hale are workers' cottages and tanning sheds.

WESLEYAN CENTENARY CELEBRATIONS, 1910. Seen passing the tannery, the Wesleyan Centenary procession is led by, left to right, Edward Garraway, George Smith and Mr Truscott. Alan Powell is to the right with the bicycle and Miss Malpas is the lady with the umbrella.

MR LIONEL MALPAS. In this unusual rural scene, coal dealer Lionel Malpas of Seven Waters is pictured together with the unlikely combination of shotgun and prize-winning sheep.

SCHOOLCHILDREN, LEONARD STANLEY, 1922. It has been possible to put names to most of these children. They are, back row, left to right: Walter Dowding, Claude Underwood, Leslie Savory, Jack Gregory, -?-, -?-, -?-, -?-, John Walker. Middle row: Ethel Price, Dorothy Large, Dorothy Stafford, Edna Bailey, Vera Osborn, Florence Anderson, Muriel Lyddiatt, Rosie ?, ? Dowding, Ida Bond. Front row: Rosie Smith, Margaret Organ, ? Gregory, -?-, Freda Smith, -?-, Annie Whitmore, Donald Clutterbuck, Gertie Cratchley (?), ? Bond, Cecil Cave. On the ground: George Lusty, ? Stockwell, -?-.

Opposite: SPIDER. Joan Organ sets off on the family pony, charmingly named Spider, from outside her cottage in Marsh Lane. Her sister Margaret and their mother look on. This picture was taken some years after the one above.

THATCHED COTTAGE, MARSH LANE. Around 1919 John Organ decided to rebuild his cottage. In this delightful photograph we see him with his wife, Ada. Daughters Joan, Edith and Margaret are sitting on the first load of bricks to arrive from Stonehouse Brick and Tile Works.

A RIDE IN A TRAP. With older girls Margaret and Joan Organ about to provide horse power, a group of children prepare to go for a ride down Marsh Lane in the Organs' trap. The date is around 1930 and the younger children are, left to right, Nancy and Edna, visitors from Wales (surname unknown), May Lusty, Joan Blick and George Lusty.

IN THE HAYFIELD. During a break in haymaking at Mr Tennyson Fawkes' field off Marsh Lane in around 1930, Wilfred Lusty (later to die at Dunkirk) is standing by the horse. May Lusty sits in the foreground with her much-loved dog. The others are, left to right, Margaret Organ, George Lusty, Pansy Lusty and Joan Organ.

HAYMAKING, 1940s. By the time of this later photograph, the Organ sisters have grown up and married. Margaret (left) is now Mrs Thomas and Edith Mrs Howard. The three children with them are Christine, Lesley and Bobby Lane. John Sayers stands behind with his bicycle.

POLISH REFUGEES IN THE STANLEYS. Jewish sisters Annelise and Illa Echt were brought by their father, a headmaster from Gdansk, to safety in England at the outset of war around 1939. Annelise (left) was billeted in Marsh Lane with the Organs, Illa at Kings Stanley post office.

CRICKET TEAM, *c.* 1910. This is believed to be the Leonard Stanley cricket team, though the only positive identification is Albert Love (second left, front row). Note the unusual pads.

LEONARD STANLEY WESLEYAN CHAPEL ANNIVERSARY, *c.* 1930. This is one of a pair of photographs and is of the congregation. Its partner (on page 7) is of the minister and visiting dignitaries.

HAYMAKING. Hay gathering still took place in the traditional way at Priory Farm in this photograph of *c.* 1940. On top of the wagon are Peter Taylor (left) and John Pullin. Audrey Pullin is astride the horse, while Frank Pullin stands by with his dog Ben.

TREE PLANTING, NEW BURIAL GROUND, GYPSY LANE. Here Miss Kitty Denison Jones plants a silver birch in the new burial ground on King George V's Silver Jubilee Day, 6 May 1935. The gentleman on the left is Mr Lapage Norris. In order to maintain ecumenical balance, Miss Peggy Wheeler from the Methodist Chapel was also invited to take part in the ceremony alongside the Anglicans.

SCHOOL CONCERT, LEONARD STANLEY. This photograph was taken around eighty years ago. The children so far identified include Olive Pearce, Phyllis Clutterbuck and Nancy Pearce (first, second and fifth from the left, back row) and Ivy Pearce, Evelyn Powell and Doris Cook (first, fifth and eighth, front row).

'THE PHOTOGRAPHER CALLS.' Taken on the lawn of The Grange are the cast of the Leonard Stanley Women's Institute play, *The Photographer Calls*, c. 1950. They are, left to right, Doris Hale (photographer), Gladys Pullin (lady-in-waiting), Miss Preedy (Queen Victoria), Joan Green (Queen's assistant) and Mrs J. Hillman (Gladstone).

THE JESTERS. This group, which was actually the church choir in another guise, performed frequently at village entertainments in the 1930s. They are, from left to right, back row: Walter Powell, Ethel Lawrence, Nora Summerfield, ? Green. Middle row: Nellie Miles, Norman Cox, Percy Blick, Vincent Summerfield, Lily Miles. Front row: Dorothy Bassett, Ida Miles.

LEONARD STANLEY PIPE BAND. This photograph, taken outside the east gate of the churchyard, dates from around 1910. It may actually show part of the Coronation celebrations mentioned earlier. The man third from the left in the bowler hat is Frank Lusty; to the right of the music is Percy Blick; far right, front row, is Mr Vaisey; and back row, on the right, with the neckerchief, is William Smith. A member of Leonard Stanley's gypsy community, Gildroy Smith, also appears on the photograph. Fourth left, back row, is Albert Love.

BRITISH LEGION PARADE. Passing down the street is a procession photographed around 1950. Far left is Col J. Norris. Others identified include Percy Gale, Frederick Morgan, William Wheeler, James Hillman and Mr Curry.

CORONATION DAY HELPERS, 1937. Among those assisting with the celebrations for King George VI's Coronation are (in alphabetical order) P. Blick, Mrs M. Bond, Ray Cave, Mabel Cook, Lily Franklin, Violet Franklin, Harry Godsell, A. Patrick, Alfred Peaple, Mrs G. Peaple, Mrs G. Pullin, Mrs J. Pullin, Mrs W. Wothers.

VE DAY, LEONARD STANLEY. The street party is in full swing as the photographer captures the moment, with Revd Chesterton wielding the teapot!

CORONATION TEA, 1953. Celebrations at Leonard Stanley included cream buns. Here a group of schoolchildren tuck in. They are, left to right: -?-, -?-, Tracey Wiltshire, Glenys Mathias (?), Peter Mathias (?), Jill Morgan, David Flagg (looking distinctly bashful), Graham Marchand, David Spencer.

LEONARD STANLEY SCHOOL CHRISTMAS PLAY, 1953. Taken, of course, in the old school, the cast of this traditional Nativity Play are, from left to right, front row: Marilyn Coleman, Margaret Squibb (?), Janet Gardiner, James Squires, David Flagg, Lesley French, Christine Powell (?), Geoffrey Harrison, Tim Brown. Kneeling behind: Carol Palk (?), Diane Herne (?), Penny Brunsdon, Gloria Davies, Mary Webb. Back row: Martin King, Mary Thomas, Diane Abel, -?-, Graham Marchand, -?-, Richard Green, Richard Griffiths, Susan Camm, Jill Morgan, David Gale, Clive Fawkes, Cyril Davis, -?-, Terry Harris.

Four

Selsley

PEAKED ELM FARM, SELSLEY. Although not a photograph, this delightful old watercolour by an unknown artist must surely merit inclusion in any pictorial study of Selsley.

Selsley, formerly a portion of Kings Stanley parish known as Stanleys End, was created a separate ecclesiastical district in June 1863. It owed its independence mainly to the mill-owning Marling family who, at the same period, built Stanley Park nearby on a superb site overlooking the Severn Valley and the mills which had been the source of their prosperity.

The foundation stone for the church was laid in 1861 and the building was consecrated in November 1862 by Rt Revd W. Thomson, Bishop of Gloucester and Archbishop Elect of York. On his travels abroad Samuel Marling had been made aware of a village in the Tyrol called Marling (or Marlengo as it became when ceded later to Italy). This, he instructed his architect G.F. Bodley, was to be the model for his design for the new church at Selsley, which explains why it looks so unlike most English Parish churches. Several generations of the Marling family have been buried there and their monuments line the south wall. However, the feature of Selsley church which makes it nationally known is its splendid series of windows, commissioned from the newly founded firm of William Morris and Co. to designs by Pre-Raphaelites Ford Maddox Brown, Rosetti, Burne-Jones and Morris himself.

Selsley was served, in the days of steam, through Dudbridge station by the much-loved 'Dudbridge Donkey', which ran to Nailsworth, Stonehouse and Stroud. There are several interesting old farmhouses in the parish, of which Peaked Elm is perhaps the finest, and a long-established and flourishing cricket team which plays on an elevated pitch in a fine position overlooking the Stonehouse valley. Of Selsley Hill, Jeptha Young of Kings Stanley wrote (perhaps rather over-enthusiastically):

> For ages Selsley Hill has stood.
> Before the fall, before the flood
> Its mightly base was laid;
> Before the sun his rays possessed
> Or drove his chariot to the west,
> It reared its lofty head.

LOOKING FROM SELSLEY TO STROUD. This fine postcard is by Mark Merrett. With Stroud in the far distance, its principal interest lies in the fields at Rodborough and Kingscourt, totally without the housing development which has since taken place there.

SELSLEY WEST. This photograph, taken one would think in high summer, shows the road through Selsley West towards Kings Stanley. The thatched cottage has now disappeared and been replaced by two bungalows.

IN A COTTAGE GARDEN. This postcard shows Mrs Herbert in the garden of the thatched cottage at Selsley West. The more familiar view of the cottage, published several times before, shows four little girls standing at the edge of the pavement.

THE HOGG FAMILY. This three-generation portrait was taken around 1915 in the garden of a cottage near the thatched one shown in the previous photographs. Mrs Higgins is seated and is with her daughter Mary Jane Hogg and grandchildren Burnal and Irene. Burnal Hogg, who died in 1986, was well-known locally, both for his photography and for his work with the scouts. Irene, now Mrs Melles, has given long service to the music at All Saints' church.

PEAKED ELM. There is an atmosphere of timelessness about this postcard view of Selsley West, taken near Peaked Elm Farm. It was discovered in a box of unidentified topographical material at a collectors' fair and dates from *c.* 1910. A cottage in the distance is remembered as Olive Marchant's sweet shop, in business in the 1920s.

HAYMAKING AT PEAKED ELM FARM, *c.* 1950. This picture looks across towards Ebley and shows, from left to right, Oliver Daniels, Harry King and Edward King.

SELSLEY CHURCH FIRE, 1916. During the afternoon of 26 April 1916, workmen employed by Gardner and Sons of King Street, Stroud, were soldering lead on the church roof when, it is thought, their blowlamp ignited a bird's nest. The whole tower was soon ablaze. Miss West, the vicar's daughter, who was in the graveyard sketching the church, helped to raise the alarm. Three fire engines attended and all furniture and valuables were removed from inside the building.

THE CHURCH CHOIR, 1930s. Photographed by the west door, the choirmen are, left to right: Mr Ross (organist), R. Capener, P. Baker, Mr Cook, Mr Herbert, Mr Gay, F. Baker, Revd H.T. Pimm; ladies: R. Griffiths, Mrs Herbert, G. Baker, V. Wade, M. Belcher, Miss Coote, L. Tarrant, M. Rogers, I. Hogg, E. Coombs.

STANLEY HALL, SELSLEY WEST. This picture dates from the 1930s and is of interest because of subsequent alterations to the gardens and the loss of the fine conservatory on the right.

ENDERLEY HOUSE, SELSLEY. Tea is served in the garden of Enderley House, which is situated near the Bell Inn and was run for many years as a guest house.

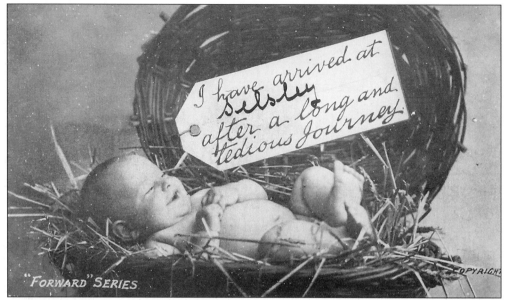

A STORK FLIES IN. This amusing postcard was sent to mark the arrival of a new member of the Cooke family at Selsley around 1910. It was, of course, a nationally produced design, with a space left for inserting a place name.

SELSLEY SCHOOL, c. 1925. The pupils' names are, left to right, back row: Ellice Stephens, Muriel Box, Winifred White, Albert Pollard, Raymond Edmonds, Edward Critchley, Sidney Summers. Second row: Gladys Long, Elsie Taylor, Doris Lusty, Dorothy Twining, Eileen Halliday, Eileen Harrison, Nancy Harrison, Nancy Turner, Irene Hogg. Third row: Herbert Wade, Geoffrey Brain, Francis Pollard, Grace Lusty, Dorothy Parker, Lulu Tritton, Dorothy Tritton, Millie White, Gladys Pollard, Jessie Brain. Front row: Edric Capener, Kenneth Summers, Dennis Belcher, Cyril Williams, Kenneth Bassett, Howard Taylor, Brian Twining, Leslie Millman, Leslie Herbert. Teacher Iris Pegler stands on the left; Kate Whiting is on the right.

SELSLEY SCHOOL, *c.* 1908. Note the children's clothes in this superb photograph, taken in front of the school a generation earlier than the last one.

SELSLEY SCOUTS, 1927. The Marlings involved themselves in all Selsley's village organizations between the wars. Standing behind the younger scouts in this Stanley Park photograph are, left to right: Herbert Dale (scout master), Tommy Herbert, Sir Percival Marling, ? Baker, Burnal Hogg and Revd Sidney Bush.

SELSLEY HILL. These old houses, fronting Selsley Hill and roughly opposite the school, have changed little since 1910, when the picture was taken. The scene is brought to life by the villagers who have come out to be photographed.

IVY COTTAGE. Taken in or around 1911, this peaceful rural view shows Ivy Cottage living up to its name. In the garden stand owners Colour Sgt William Butler and his wife Alice.

VILLAGE WEDDING. This family portrait is taken in the garden of Ivy Cottage. The marriage is that of Walter Daniels Lusty and Edith Grace Foster. In the background, resplendent in his military uniform, is Colour Sgt Butler.

AT THE GARDEN GATE. Here a visitor from Leicester holds the hand of Miss Doris Lusty. The picture dates from around 1920. Note the hat, then no doubt the height of fashion.

DUDBRIDGE STATION. This detailed late Edwardian postcard of Dudbridge Midland Railway Junction Station is of excellent quality. It is by E.P. Conway of Nailsworth.

DUDBRIDGE STATION CLOSE-UP. Part of the brick retaining wall and platform on the right may now be seen preserved near the new roundabout at the bottom of Selsley Hill. Note the station furniture and the reused railway carriage which served as a canteen for link men and porters.

STATION STAFF, DUDBRIDGE. Taken from a small, informal snapshot, this photograph shows the station staff at Dudbridge around 1926.

KIMMINS MILL, DUDBRIDGE, 1920s. In the foreground is Jefferies' coal yard. Miss Eileen Halliday recalls that Russian grain, arriving for the mill, would be off-loaded in the warehouse on the right into flat trucks and taken across the bridge straight into the mill. Power was normally provided by the water-wheel just visible to the left of the building, though, when needed, trucks of anthracite, as shown, could be diverted off the siding across the same bridge to provide an alternative source of energy. Note the mill's Flemish chimney, so-called because, together with a handful of others in the area, it was built by Huguenot craftsmen.

ELEPHANTS AT DUDBRIDGE. This small, rather faded photograph dating from around the 1950s, shows Bertram Mills' circus elephants, recently arrived at Dudbridge station, heading off to parade around Stroud before reaching Victory Park, Cainscross, where they were to perform. The story is told that, some years before, a similar group of elephants, disembarking at Dudbridge station, were spotted from Stanley Park Lower Lodge by Mr Percy Smith, deputy head gardener to Sir Percival and Lady Marling. What actually attracted Mr Smith's attention was not so much the animals themselves as the sizeable offerings left behind by them in the road. Hastening out with wheelbarrow and spade, he rescued this outsize windfall to feed his garden. What effect such a rich mixture had on the plants is, sadly, not recorded!

HAYMAKING AT SELSLEY. Many good photographs of haymaking have survived for Selsley parish. In this first picture, probably taken around 1910, Albert and Lily Griffiths stand, right, with their children Rose and Raymond.

RICK CONSTRUCTION. This second haymaking scene shows an early stage of rick building, with Albert Griffiths on the right.

ANOTHER LOAD ARRIVES. In the third haymaking scene, at Stanley Park Farm, Mr Clinch from Home Farm stands nearest to the horse. Next to him is Bill Brunsdon, then Fred Ashmead and Fred Clinch. The picture was taken in the 1930s.

CORONATION BONFIRE, 1911. The 1911 Selsley bonfire scene is well-known but is considered too important to omit from this collection. Sir William H. Marling is fifth from the left. The bonfire was in the charge of Mr Ephraim Claridge and the principal helpers in its construction were Edward King, Fred White and Walter Lusty. It measured, when complete, 35 ft tall and 17 ft in diameter. Earlier on Coronation day there had been a church service, a dinner at Stanley Park for the over-60s, (with the Royal Toast given by Sir William) and a procession with floats. When the latter reached Stanley Park, white doves were released, a tea was held and sports followed. Conjuring and the planting of an oak tree took place later.

THE 1937 CORONATION BONFIRE. King George VI's Coronation in June 1937 provided another opportunity for a bonfire on Selsley Common, the King family, as usual, taking a leading role. Harry is in the light coat in the centre, with son Edward holding a length of timber just in front of him. Many other Selsley names are represented, including Harrison, Millman, Steele, Turner, Belcher, Kilmister, Lusty, Dangerfield, Wyman and Evans. Amongst the group of young helpers are Eric Lusty, Jack Durn and Curly Williams. The familiar figure of Burnal Hogg can be seen far left.

THE 1953 CORONATION BONFIRE. Here we see the partway stage in the construction of this bonfire. From the left are Les Baker, Harry Steele, Stuart Millman, Harry King (the Kings were, as we have seen, regular and enthusiastic bonfire builders) and Mrs Elliott. Amongst those on the right are Jack Lusty, Jack Durn and Les Millman.

SELSLEY FOOTBALL TEAM, c. 1920. The players are as follows. Back row: Stan Williams, Archie Harrison, Stan Cook. Middle row: -?-, Arthur Heskins, Alf Cook. Front row: Reg Sharp, Arthur Ashmead, Bernard Dent, Bert King, -?-.

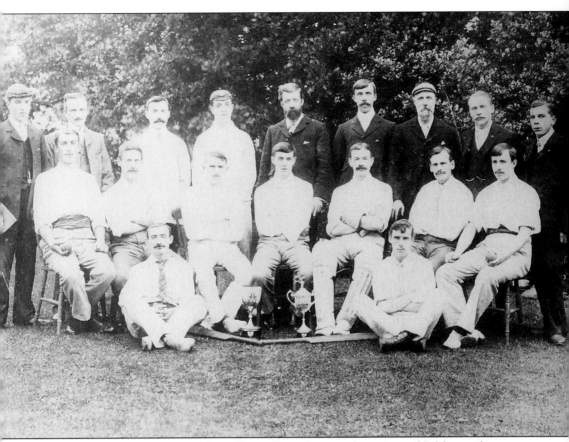

SELSLEY CRICKET CLUB, 1905. Several excellent photographs survive of Selsley cricketers. For many years the club, based at its attractive ground part way up Selsley Hill, boasted a 1st and a 2nd XI. This picture shows the 1st XI in 1905, when they won the Stroud and District Challenge Cup. They are, back row, left to right: F. Millman (scorer), H.E. Solomon (Hon. Treas.), E. Baker, G.P. Hague, H. Dangerfield, C. Elliott, S. Hague, R. Smith (umpire), C. Baker. Middle row: A. Browning, M. Cordwell, T. Griffiths (Hon. Sec.), T. Summers (capt.), J. Harper (vice capt.), G. Harrison, F. Elliott. Seated on the ground: E. Swaine, A. Ashmead.

SELSLEY JAZZ BAND. In this 1930s postcard the Selsley Jazz Band is seen aboard a splendidly decorated horse-drawn float, ready to set out for Stroud Show. A collector's tray reveals that funds are being raised for Stroud Hospital. Those on the float include members of the Hogg, Baker, Knight, Elliott, Cratchley and Summers families.

A FANCY-DRESS GROUP. This photograph may possibly represent carnival entries for the 1919 Peace celebrations. The participants are, left to right, Mrs Nellie Harrison, Miss R. Herbert, Mrs Nell Summers, Mrs Lucy Harrison and, in front, Nancy Harrison.

CHARABANC TRIP, STANLEY END. Where this fine body of men were heading is unclear, but the picture is believed to show a pub outing assembled near the Bell Inn in the early 1920s. Those identified are: back row, far left, Ted May; fourth left, Sidney Summers. Front row: -?-, -?-, -?-, -?-, Victor Box, Albert Griffiths, Arthur Williams, John Belcher, Archie Harrison, -?-, -?-, -?-, Harry Herbert. The gentleman on the far right must surely take the prize for the most unusual nickname: he is remembered as 'Gunboat' Smith, though his real name was Fred.

SKITTLES AT THE NEW INN. This ancient hostelry stood on Selsley Common, on the left going up, just past where the cattle grid is now positioned. It was unusual in that it had an open-air skittle alley. Here, in a picture dateable to around 1950, Mrs Summers tries her hand at bowling. The landlord, Ernest Cratchley, is seen nearest to the fence on the left, while the vicar, Revd Habgood, looks on from a vantage point in front of the inn sign on the right.

THE GARDENS AT STANLEY
PARK: TWO CONTRASTING
VIEWS. The following photographs are
intended to illustrate social life at
Stanley Park in the 1920s and 1930s.
They come, with the family's kind
permission, from Sir Percival and Lady
Marling's private collection. The first
pair are views of the garden facade at
different seasons of the year.

Opposite: AT A
ROYAL GARDEN
PARTY. An
invitation to a
Buckingham Palace
Garden Party was the
high point in the
social calendar of all
county families. Here
Sir Percival and Lady
Marling are seen at
the Palace in the
summer of 1933.
Royal princes hover to
the left and King
George V strolls off
with hat in hand
while the Marlings
wait for Queen Mary
to turn and speak.

THE GARDENS, *c.* 1940. In the immaculate grounds of Stanley Park there were, naturally, many flower borders. The one in the foreground of this view, it is recalled, frequently contained, by Lady Marling's special request, a spring arrangement of red tulips and forget-me-nots.

INTERIOR, STANLEY PARK. As the family album makes plain, Stanley Park was the scene of a varied series of events seventy years ago. There were fancy-dress balls, parties and, above all, great seasonal festivities at Christmas. Sir Percival's sister-in-law, Helen Marling from Great Rissington, often came to stay and would pen a poem for inclusion in the album. Her offering for Christmas 1928 began:

> Where is it where from troubles free,
> So full of fun and jollity,
> We all at Christmas love to be?
> At Stanley Park.
>
> Where is it where the drink's so good
> And there is lots of luscious food
> (An absolutely priceless pud!)?
> At Stanley Park.
>
> Where are we always sure to find
> Welcoming smiles and servants kind,
> With warmth for body, peace for mind?
> At Stanley Park.
>
> Where is the party of the best,
> Tea, tree and plays, with many a jest
> And presents for each lucky guest?
> At Stanley Park.

MENU

CHAUD:

Consommé Brunoise.

———

Côtelettes de Mouton aux Haricots verts.

———:o:———

FROID:

Filets de Soles Nantua.

Suprême de Volaille Moncey.

Mazarin de Jambon Hongroise.

Chaudfroid de Faisan.

———

Salade en Saison.

———

Pâté de Gibier.

Poulet rôti et bouilli découpé.

Jambon de York.

Langue de Bœuf.

———

Gelées aux Bananas.

Macédoine de Fruits.

Meringues Chantilly.

Pâtisserie.

STANLEY PARK.   January 2nd, 1924

SILVER WEDDING CELEBRATIONS. In January 1924 Sir Percival and Lady Beatrice Marling marked their silver wedding with a fancy dress ball at Stanley Park. Judging from the menu and dance card it was quite an occasion!

PROGR

Dances.

1	ONE-STEP	...	...	Toot, Toot, Tootsie
2	FOX-TROT	...	...	My Sweetie went away
3	WALTZ ...	...	...	Just for a while
4	FOX-TROT	...	...	... Moon Love
5	FOX-TROT	...	...	Dancing Honeymoon
6	VALTZ ...	...	...	Wonderful One
7	FOX-TROT	...	...	... Chansonette
8	VALTZ ...	...	...	... The Merry Widow

EXTRAS.   SUPPER.

9	IX-TROT	...	...	... Dearest
10	ALTZ ...	...	...	... Marcheta
11	FOX-TROT	...	...	Aggravatin' Papa
12	VALSE COTILLON	...	...	...
13	WALTZ ...	...	Three o'clock in the morning
14	FOX-TROT	...	...	Runnin' Wild
15	FOX-TROT	...	...	... Dumbell
16	WALTZ ...	...	...	A Kiss in the Dark
17	FOX-TROT	...	...	Oh Gee. Oh Gosh
18	POST HORN GALOP	...	...	...

CLIFFORD

STANLEY PARK.

———

FANCY DRESS BALL.

———

January 2nd, 1924.

125

ENTERTAINING, 1934. Here Lady Marling hosts an outing for girls from the Bussage House of Mercy. The local newspaper records that she 'arranged for tea to be partaken on the terrace. After tea, Mr Tom Waterman, whose hand is certainly quick enough to deceive the eye, entertained the visitors with a display of conjuring. The girls joined in competitions arranged by Lady Marling and, before they left, each received a present!' Shades of a vanished age ...

MEET OF THE BERKELEY HOUNDS, STANLEY PARK, 1933. Present at the meet were many local dignitaries, including Sir Stanley Tubbs of Wotton-under-Edge and Captain Graham-Clarke of Frocester. As the picture shows, there was also a sizeable crowd of hunt followers.

THE FOUNTAIN. This second pair of
contrasting views shows the main garden
fountain at Christmas 1925 and again
during the summer of 1937.

THE END OF AN ERA. Lady Beatrice Marling died aged eighty in July 1941, only three months after the royal visit. She and Sir Percival had been devoted to each other. His autobiography, *Rifleman and Hussar*, concludes with the words, 'And above all, I thank God for a good wife.' Here her funeral cortège is seen in the grounds of Stanley Park, passing the lowered banners of the organizations to which she had given unstinting support over the years. A youthful Philip Ford, the undertaker (right), leads the procession, with colleague Mr Anthony on his right. Walton, the head gardener, pulls the coffin, assisted by Percy Smith, his deputy, and gardeners Reg Cook and Arthur Heskins.

Acknowledgements

Many friends and acquaintances – both old and new – have given help and advice or lent material for this book. To all of them I am most grateful, but especially to Peter Griffin who has not only made available his photographic collection, but also patiently assisted in the identification of problematical pictures. Amongst those who have also willingly co-operated in my researches are: J. Anderson, Mrs B. Baker, Mrs M. Birkin, D. Burton, Mrs N. Clarke, Mrs S. Cooke, D. Cope, E. Cuss, D. Flagg, P. Ford, Mrs D. Gardiner, Mrs E. Gardiner, S. Gardiner, Mrs R. Gibson, Mrs F. Gittos, Mrs I. Griffin, P. Griffiths, Mrs G. Haines, Mrs D. Hale, J. Hale, Miss E. Halliday, P. Harris, A. Holley, Mrs M. Hoy, Mrs J. Hudson, A. Iles, A. Kardynal, Mrs V. Kilmister, Mrs M. King, Mrs B. Lusty, the Misses D. and G. Lusty, E. Lusty, Sir Charles Marling, B. Mayo, Mrs I. Melles, W. Merrett, S. Mills, B. Moss, Mrs M. Payne, J. Pullin, D. Ring, F. Rowbotham, F. Smith and Wycliffe College, P. Sturm, K. Summers, Mrs M. Thomas, E. Wheeler, E. White, Mrs G. Wright.

Finally, my grateful thanks to my wife, Sylvia, for her constant help, advice and encouragement.